A Good Friend

Written by

Rob Waring and **Maurice Jamall**

Before You Read

to carry 

to cut 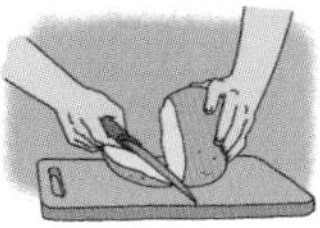

beach 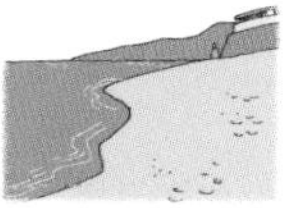

bottle 

foot 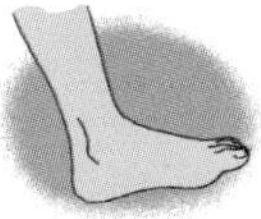

forest 

guitar 

hospital 

hurt 

jacket 

sun 

surprised 

worried 

In the story

Eric

Yoko

Mrs. Ogawa

"Do you want to come?" asks Eric. Eric is at his friend Yoko's house. He and Yoko often go to the beach.
"I'm going down to the beach again. I want to watch the sun go down and sing some songs. We'll have a great time," he says.
"Can you come?" he asks.
"Thanks, Eric. Yeah, I want to come," she says. "I'll ask my mom."
She's very excited.

Yoko talks to her mother about Eric.
"Can I go?" Yoko asks her mother.
Mrs. Ogawa looks at Eric. She says, "No. I don't like him. His hair is too long. I don't like that kind of boy. And you are too young for a boyfriend."
"But Mom, he's *not* my boyfriend," says Yoko. "Eric is really nice! It'll be okay, Mom. Please!"
"No!" Mrs. Ogawa says. "No, you can't go out! You have a test tomorrow."

Yoko talks to Eric. "I'm sorry, Eric. I can't go. I have a test tomorrow. Mom wants me to study," she says.
Eric understands. "Oh, I see," he says.
Yoko says, "I'm really sorry, Eric. I really want to come with you."
Eric says, "It's okay. I'll see you at school tomorrow. Bye."
"Yeah. Bye," says Yoko.

Later, Yoko goes back to her room. Yoko doesn't want to study. She wants to be with Eric on the beach.
"I want to see the sun go down," she thinks. "And sing some songs, too."
Yoko thinks about Eric for a long time.
She thinks, "I'm going to see Eric."

Yoko does not tell her mother she wants to go to the beach.
"Mom," she says. "I don't want dinner tonight. I want to study for tomorrow's test, and then go to sleep," she says.
Yoko's mother is very surprised. "You never study for tests, and it's only 6 o'clock," she says.
Yoko says, "Good night!"
"Oh, okay. Good night, Yoko," says her mother.
Yoko goes back to her room. But she does not study. She goes out of her window. She wants to see Eric!

Yoko rides to the beach on her bike.
"Hi, Eric," she says. Yoko smiles at him.
"Yoko!" he says. He is very surprised. "Why are you here?"
Yoko tells him about her mother, and about her lie.
Eric says, "That's not good, Yoko."
"I know," says Yoko. "But I want to see the sun go down with you, Eric."
Eric says, "Your mother will be worried. I'm taking you back home now."

"No, Eric," says Yoko. "I want to sing some songs."
Eric takes her back to her bike. He does not listen to her.
Yoko then says, "Ouch!"
"What's wrong, Yoko?" Eric asks.
"My foot hurts," she says. "The bottle cut my foot."
Eric looks at the bottle. He says, "Oh, no! Are you okay?"
"No, I can't walk," she says.

Yoko cannot ride her bike. They do not have a phone. They cannot call for help. Nobody can help them.
"Yoko, I'll help you get home," says Eric.
Yoko replies, "But what about the bikes, and your guitar?"
"Let's leave the bikes and guitar here," he says. "I'll get them tomorrow."
Eric helps Yoko. She is heavy and it is hard work.

"Eric, I'm sorry," she says. "I can't walk any more. My foot hurts."

Eric carries Yoko a long way. The sun is going down.

Eric says, "I can't go for help and leave you here. I want to take you to the hospital," he says. "Let's keep walking."

"Thanks Eric," she says. "I'm really sorry."

"It's very dark," says Yoko. "I can't see."
"Don't worry, Yoko. I'll help you," says Eric.
Eric says, "Yoko, here, you can have my jacket. You're cold," he says.
He gives Yoko his jacket. "Thanks, Eric," she says. "You're so kind. And you're a good friend."
Then it starts to rain. They start walking again.

It is now 10:30. Yoko's mother goes to Yoko's room to say goodnight. But Yoko is not there. She is not in bed. Mrs. Ogawa looks all over the house.

"Oh no!" thinks Mrs. Ogawa. "Where's Yoko?" She is very worried.

Then she hears the phone. It's Eric.

"Hello, Mrs. Ogawa. This is Eric," he says. "I'm at the hospital with Yoko. Please come."

Mrs. Ogawa goes to the hospital.

Mrs. Ogawa is very happy to see Yoko again.
"Yoko, are you okay?" she asks.
"I'm fine now, but my foot hurts," she says. "Mom, I'm really sorry."
"That's okay," her mother says. "You are okay now."
Mrs. Ogawa thinks Eric is bad because Yoko is hurt. She does not know about Yoko's lie. She does not know about Eric's help.
"Eric, I'm really angry with you. Don't ask Yoko to go to the beach again," she says.

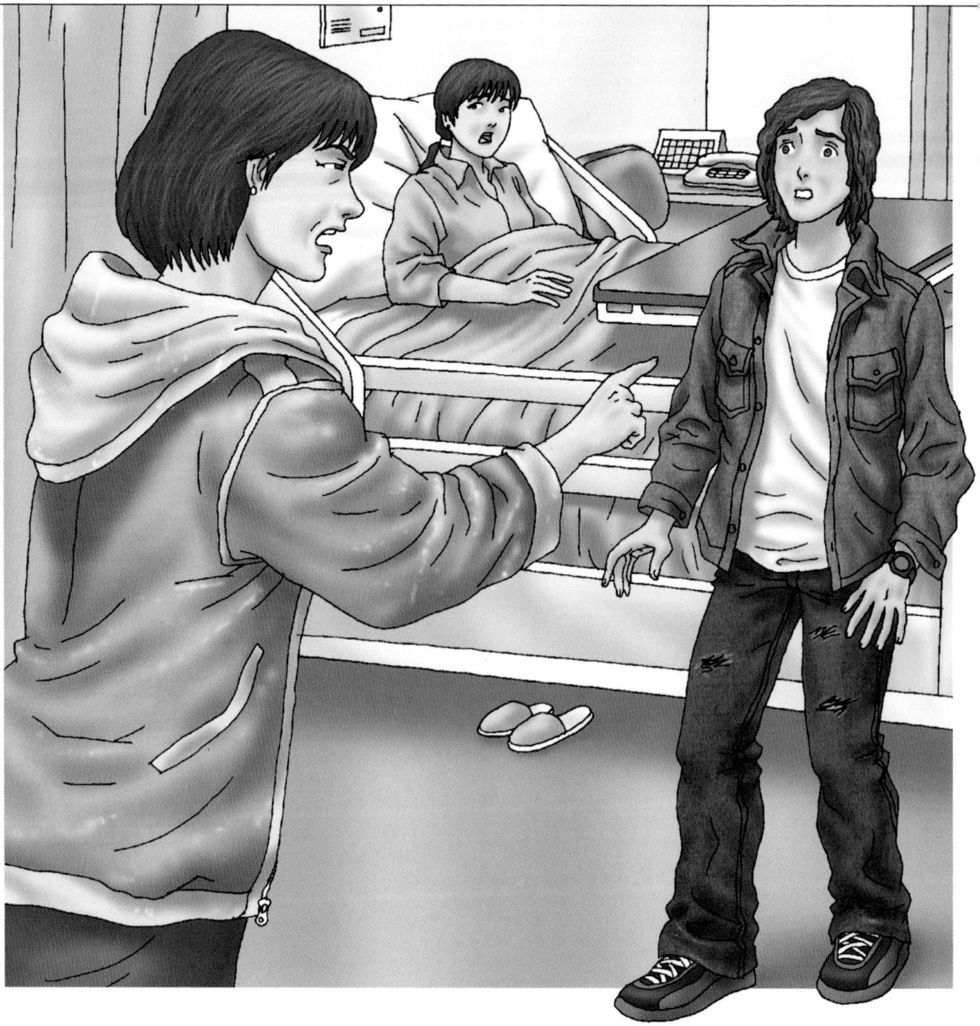

Yoko says, "But, Mom, Eric is not the bad one. I'm the bad one."
"Why?" Mrs. Ogawa asks. "Tell me about tonight, Yoko. I want to know everything!"
Yoko tells her Mom about the lie, the bottle, and about Eric's help.
"Oh, I see," she says. "Well, thank you, Eric. I'm sorry, Eric. You are a good friend to Yoko."

Yoko's mother goes home.
"I'm going home now," says Eric. "My parents will be worried. I'll come and see you tomorrow after the test."
Yoko says, "Thanks again, Eric. You're a good friend."
"That's okay," he replies.
He looks at her and smiles. He says, "You are more than a good friend to me."